Dream-Eater's Guide to Wealth

Dream-Eater's Guide to Wealth

Matthew Petchinsky

1

Dream-Eater's Guide to Wealth

By: Matthew Petchinsky

DISCLAIMER

This book presents real metaphysical practices, symbolic frameworks, and intentional consciousness techniques. It is not a work of fiction.

Dream-Eater's Guide to Wealth is a metaphysical and symbolic magickal text intended for adults who consciously choose to engage with inner psychological, energetic, and symbolic systems related to desire, scarcity, fear, ambition, and wealth consciousness. The practices, language, and structures presented herein operate at the level of **meaning, intention, pattern interruption, subconscious reprogramming, and symbolic interaction with the psyche and energetic field**.

This book does **not** claim to override natural law, guarantee financial outcomes, replace professional advice, or bypass effort, ethics, or responsibility.

No Guarantees of Financial Outcome

Results described or implied in this book are **not guaranteed**. Wealth, abundance, and financial stability are influenced by many factors, including but not limited to personal decisions, environment, economic conditions, skills, access, timing, and sustained action. Any references to wealth are **symbolic, directional, and consciousness-based**, not promises of specific monetary gain.

Not Financial, Legal, or Medical Advice

Nothing in this book should be interpreted as:

- Financial advice
- Investment advice
- Legal advice
- Medical or psychological treatment

Readers are encouraged to consult qualified professionals for financial planning, legal matters, mental health care, or medical concerns. This text operates in the **symbolic and metaphysical domain**, not the professional advisory domain.

Psychological & Emotional Responsibility

Some practices in this book may surface **deep emotional material**, including fear, scarcity patterns, internalized shame, or unconscious beliefs around money and power. These experiences are part of **inner awareness work**, not a substitute for therapy.

If at any time the reader experiences distress, dissociation, anxiety, or emotional instability, they are advised to **pause engagement with the material** and seek appropriate support.

Personal Sovereignty & Consent

By reading and engaging with this book, the reader affirms:

- They are participating **voluntarily**
- They retain full personal sovereignty
- They accept responsibility for how they interpret and apply the material

The author does not assume responsibility for misuse, misinterpretation, or application beyond the reader's personal capacity or ethical framework.

Symbolic Language & Non-Literal Entities

Any references to "dream-eaters," forces, currents, entities, or mechanisms are **symbolic constructs** used to describe internal and energetic processes. They are not presented as external beings requiring belief, worship, or fear. The language is **functional, not dogmatic**.

No allegiance, devotion, or submission is requested or required.

Ethical Use Clause

This book is intended for **self-development, awareness, empowerment, and ethical wealth consciousness**. It is not designed to manipulate, exploit, coerce, harm, or dominate others. Any attempt to use these concepts to intentionally cause harm, deception, or exploitation falls outside the purpose of this work.

No Religious Affiliation

This book is **not affiliated with any religion**, religious doctrine, or organized belief system. It does not reference, rely upon, or promote Christianity, Judaism, Islam, or any institutional religious framework.

Energetic Responsibility Statement

Magick, as presented here, is the disciplined use of attention, meaning, intention, and pattern recognition. The reader accepts full responsibility for how they engage with their inner world, beliefs, and actions as influenced by this material.

If you proceed, you do so as a conscious participant—not a passive recipient.

This book does not command. It invites.

Introduction

Wealth begins where nightmares end.

Most people attempt to build wealth by chasing daylight—budgets, affirmations, hustle, and surface-level optimism—while their true financial fate is being decided at night. In dreams. In fear. In the unprocessed images the mind buries and the body remembers.

Poverty is not sustained by lack of effort.
It is sustained by **unfed fear**.

Every recurring nightmare, intrusive thought, money panic, and survival fantasy carries energy. When that energy is ignored, it turns inward and corrodes decision-making, confidence, timing, and risk tolerance. When it is consumed, transmuted, and metabolized, it becomes fuel.

This is where the Dream-Eater enters.

The Dream-Eater is not a myth, a superstition, or a story device. It is an **astral archetype**—a functional construct that operates within the liminal space between subconscious fear and conscious action. Its role is simple and precise: **to consume fear at its source and convert it into usable power**, specifically power related to survival, resource flow, and prosperity.

This book does not teach you to suppress fear.
It teaches you to **feed it.**

Why Fear Is the Gatekeeper of Wealth

Fear governs money more than logic ever will. Fear decides whether you:

- Ask for more
- Charge correctly
- Invest wisely
- Leave unsafe situations
- Recognize opportunity when it appears

Fear is not an enemy. It is a resource that has been mishandled.

The modern world teaches people to "heal" fear, "release" fear, or "rise above" fear. Those methods often fail because fear does not want to be erased—it wants to be **used**. When fear is denied, it mutates into avoidance, paralysis, and self-sabotage. When fear is consumed properly, it becomes clarity, instinct, and precision.

The Dream-Eater is the mechanism by which this consumption occurs.

Forgotten Dreamwork as Wealth Alchemy

Before money was numbers, it was survival imagery.
Before markets, there were dreams of famine, abundance, shelter, and dominance. The human nervous system still operates on these ancient symbols, regardless of how modern the economy appears.

This book revives **forgotten dreamwork techniques**—not for escapism, but for practical transformation. You will learn how to:

- Identify fear-rich dream material
- Invoke the Dream-Eater as an internal consuming force
- Redirect nightmare energy into waking-world advantage
- Break inherited poverty patterns encoded in sleep imagery
- Reprogram scarcity at the level where it is generated

This is not visualization.
This is **metabolic dream magick**.

Financial Invincibility Is Not Wealth—It Is Immunity

To be financially invincible does not mean never losing money. It means never being **psychologically destroyed** by loss. It means fear no longer dictates your reactions, decisions, or identity.

When fear is eaten instead of avoided:

- Failure becomes information
- Risk becomes calculated
- Money stops carrying emotional charge
- Opportunity becomes visible

The Dream-Eater does not make you reckless. It makes you **unshakeable**.

Who This Book Is For

This work is for those who:

- Have worked hard but feel blocked by invisible limits
- Experience anxiety, dread, or paralysis around money
- Sense that their financial patterns are older than their choices
- Are willing to engage with the subconscious rather than deny it
- Understand that real power comes from integration, not denial

This book is **not** for passive readers. It requires attention, honesty, and participation.

What This Book Will Ask of You

You will be asked to:

- Enter your own dream material without judgment
- Face fear directly, without romanticizing it
- Use symbolic and energetic frameworks responsibly
- Accept sovereignty over your financial psyche

Nothing in this book will override your free will.
Nothing in this book will work without consent.

A Final Threshold

The Dream-Eater does not arrive to save you.
It arrives when you are ready to stop wasting fear.

If you proceed, you are choosing to end the cycle where nightmares drain you and begin the cycle where they **feed you**.

Wealth begins where nightmares end.
Turn the page when you are ready to eat.

CHAPTER 1 — The Sleep Debt Curse

Sleep Is Not Rest—It Is Resource Processing

Sleep has been falsely framed as recovery, a pause, a shutdown. In truth, sleep is the **primary processing chamber for survival data**. While the waking mind manages tasks, the sleeping mind audits threat, safety, loss, and future viability. Every night, the psyche sorts images tied to food, shelter, power, exclusion, and security. When this process is interrupted, ignored, or suppressed, the system does not stop working—it begins storing unresolved material as pressure.

Chronic exhaustion is rarely caused by lack of sleep alone. It is caused by **unfinished dream labor**. When fear-heavy dreams are dismissed as "just dreams," the psyche carries that unprocessed fear forward into waking life. This manifests as decision fatigue, financial hesitation, overwork without payoff, and the persistent sense that effort never equals reward. The body remains tired because the mind never completed its night work.

Wealth stagnation often coincides with disrupted dream processing. The nervous system interprets unresolved fear as ongoing threat, even when the external environment appears stable. This keeps the body in conservation mode—risk-averse, contraction-based, and hyper-vigilant. Money decisions made from this state prioritize survival over growth, safety over expansion, familiarity over opportunity.

To awaken from the Sleep Debt Curse, the reader must abandon the belief that dreams are disposable. Dreams are **transactions**. When they are not completed, debt accumulates—not financial debt, but energetic debt that quietly dictates behavior, tolerance, and perceived limits.

Fear Density Markers: How to Recognize Valuable Dream Material

Not all dreams matter equally. Some are surface noise—memory fragments, sensory echoes, unfinished conversations. Others are **fear-dense**, carrying compressed survival energy. These dreams repeat, linger emotionally, or return with minor variations. They are not random. They are signals that something essential was not metabolized.

Fear-rich dreams often share specific markers. Recurring locations indicate unresolved territory—places the psyche cannot exit because meaning remains trapped there. Being chased, trapped, or watched reveals a power imbalance that has not been resolved internally. Money-loss imagery—stolen wallets, unpaid bills, empty accounts—points directly to scarcity coding. Broken shelter, empty stores, or missing resources signal perceived future threat, regardless of present circumstances.

The emotional residue matters more than the storyline. A dream that "felt wrong" hours after waking is more valuable than a vivid dream that evaporated. Fear density is measured by **stickiness**, not drama. If the body remembers it, the system is still holding it.

These dreams are not warnings of doom. They are **containers of stored energy**. The mistake most people make is attempting to interpret them intellectually or dismiss them emotionally. Fear-rich dreams do not want explanation—they want consumption.

Dream Triage: Separating Signal from Noise

Without triage, dreamwork becomes overwhelming or meaningless. The Dream Triage System exists to prevent both. It teaches the reader to sort dreams by function, not symbolism. The question is not "What does this mean?" but "Does this carry fear energy that affects my waking behavior?"

Dreams that must be recorded meet at least one of the following criteria: they repeat; they involve loss, pursuit, exposure, or deprivation; they produce lingering emotion; or they alter mood upon waking. These dreams are active. They are still drawing power.

Dreams that feed scarcity often masquerade as mundane stress dreams—being late, missing something important, failing a task repeatedly. These dreams encode the belief that effort does not result in safety or reward. Over time, they train the nervous system to expect collapse even during progress.

Noise dreams dissipate quickly and leave no residue. They do not alter behavior, mood, or decision-making. Recording them is optional. The system does not benefit from hoarding meaningless data.

Triage restores authority. The reader stops drowning in dreams and starts **selecting fuel**.

Fear Is Stored Energy, Not a Flaw

Fear is not evidence of weakness. It is evidence of **stored survival charge**. When fear is labeled pathology, it is suppressed. When it is treated as energy, it becomes usable. Every nightmare contains compressed attention, heightened clarity, and instinctual focus—qualities essential for wealth creation.

The problem is not fear itself, but misplacement. Fear that remains unfed leaks into waking life as overthinking, avoidance, people-pleasing, undercharging, and exhaustion. It becomes background radiation rather than directed force.

By reframing fear as stored energy, the reader reclaims agency. Nightmares are no longer intrusions; they are **deliveries**. Each one brings raw material that can be processed, consumed, and converted.

This chapter marks the shift from avoidance to extraction. Fear is no longer something to escape. It is something to **harvest**.

RITUAL — The Sleep Debt Audit

Purpose: To identify accumulated dream debt and mark fear-rich material for harvesting.

Steps:

1. Choose three consecutive mornings. Do not attempt interpretation during this ritual.
2. Upon waking, remain still for one full minute. Allow images to surface without forcing recall.
3. Write down only fragments that carry emotional charge—locations, sensations, or threats.
4. Circle any recurring element across the three days.
5. Declare aloud: *"This fear is accounted for. It will no longer leak."*
6. Close the ritual by placing the notes somewhere visible during the day.

EXERCISE 1 — Fear Density Mapping

Step 1: Select one recorded dream.

Step 2: List every element that involved loss, pursuit, or exposure.

Step 3: Rate each element's emotional intensity from 1–10.

Step 4: Identify the highest-rated element. This is the core fuel source.

EXERCISE 2 — Waking Leak Detection

Step 1: Observe one financial decision you avoid or delay.

Step 2: Trace the emotion underneath the hesitation.

Step 3: Match that emotion to a recent dream image.

Step 4: Record the connection without judgment.

EXERCISE 3 — Noise Elimination

Step 1: Review five recent dreams.

Step 2: Cross out any dream with no lingering emotion.

Step 3: Notice the relief created by removal.

Step 4: Commit to recording only fear-dense material going forward.

CHARM — The Night Ledger Sigil
Purpose: To prevent unprocessed fear from carrying into the day.
Steps:

1. Draw a simple symbol representing containment (circle, box, gate).
2. Place it beside your bed.
3. Before sleep, touch the symbol and say: *"What appears tonight will be held."*
4. Upon waking, touch it again to signal closure.

SPELL 1 — Naming the Debt

Purpose: To prevent fear from silently compounding into exhaustion, avoidance, and financial hesitation.

Timing: Immediately upon waking, before checking time, phone, or speaking to anyone.

Step 1 — Stillness Before Language

Remain completely still when you wake. Do not stretch. Do not sit up. Let the body stay exactly as it is. This prevents the fear charge from dispersing into unconscious movement.

Step 2 — Locate the Residue

Scan the body slowly and identify where the dream's emotion still lives. Common locations include the chest, throat, stomach, jaw, or behind the eyes. Do not analyze the dream—only locate the sensation.

Step 3 — Name Without Story

Silently name the emotion in one word only (fear, dread, urgency, loss, pressure). Do not add narrative. This isolates the energy from imagination.

Step 4 — Spoken Accounting

Now speak aloud, slowly and clearly:

"This fear is counted. It will not compound."

Say it once with full attention. The voice marks the fear as *recorded*, not ignored.

Step 5 — Physical Seal

Exhale through the mouth and gently press your tongue to the roof of your mouth for three seconds. This signals closure to the nervous system.

Effect:

Fear is logged instead of leaking. The psyche no longer treats it as unresolved debt that must collect interest throughout the day.

SPELL 2 — Ending Leakage

Purpose: To stop unresolved fear from spilling into dreams as repetitive stress imagery.

Timing: Performed every night before sleep, even on "good" days.

Step 1 — Threshold Creation

Sit or stand beside your bed. Place one hand on the bedframe or mattress. This marks the physical boundary between waking and sleep.

Step 2 — Inventory Without Judgment

Briefly scan the day and notice any moment that caused tension, avoidance, or financial stress. Do not solve anything. Simply acknowledge that something remains open.

Step 3 — Containment Gesture

Imagine placing those unresolved moments into a sealed container—box, vault, or shadowed room. The form does not matter; the sense of containment does.

Step 4 — Spoken Boundary

Say aloud, clearly and firmly:

"Nothing unresolved crosses the threshold."

Say it once. Do not repeat. Repetition weakens authority.

Step 5 — Sleep Entry

Lie down immediately after speaking. Do not scroll, think, or revisit the day. Allow the boundary to hold.

Effect:

Dreams shift from chaotic replay to **structured fear delivery**, making them easier to harvest instead of endure.

SPELL 3 — Claiming the Harvest

Purpose: To convert fear-rich dream energy into usable power instead of emotional drain.

Timing: After writing down a fear-rich dream.

Step 1 — Record First, Always

Write the dream before speaking the spell. Even fragments count. Writing anchors the energy so it does not dissipate or turn into rumination.

Step 2 — Identify the Core Fear

Underline the single moment in the dream where fear peaked. Not the whole dream—only the sharpest point.

Step 3 — Physical Contact

Place your hand over the body area that reacted most strongly in the dream (chest, stomach, throat). This grounds the energy.

Step 4 — Spoken Conversion

Say aloud, slowly:

"What frightened me now feeds me."

Pause for a full breath after speaking.

Step 5 — Visualization of Consumption

Briefly imagine the fear being drawn inward and broken down—like fuel entering an engine or heat entering a furnace. Do not imagine destruction; imagine **use**.

Step 6 — Immediate Action Anchor

Within one hour, take a small decisive action related to money, boundaries, or planning. This teaches the system that fear now results in movement, not paralysis.

Effect:

Nightmares stop draining energy and begin supplying clarity, decisiveness, and momentum.

MEDITATION — The Still Waking Gate
Steps:

1. Sit upright immediately after waking.
2. Close your eyes and breathe slowly for ten counts.
3. Visualize a gate closing behind you, sealing the dream world.
4. Sense any remaining emotion being drawn inward, not outward.
5. Open your eyes only when the sensation stabilizes.

JOURNAL PROMPTS

1. Which dreams repeat most often?
2. What emotion lingers longest after waking?
3. Where does fear show up in my financial behavior?
4. Which dream images feel older than my current life?
5. What do I avoid immediately after waking?
6. How does my body respond to scarcity thoughts?
7. Which fears feel inherited rather than chosen?
8. What changes when I record instead of dismiss?
9. How much energy is tied up in unprocessed dreams?
10. What would happen if fear became fuel?

Closing Reflection

The Sleep Debt Curse is not punishment. It is backlog. Nothing here has gone wrong—nothing has been wasted. Your nightmares were never enemies; they were unpaid labor waiting to be claimed. From this moment forward, you are no longer haunted by what you ignore. You are strengthened by what you collect. The night has begun working *for* you.

CHAPTER 2 — Nightmares as Portals

Nightmares Are Access Points, Not Errors

Nightmares are not glitches in the mind's operating system. They are **intentional pressure releases** triggered when fear energy reaches a concentration too dense to remain buried. When the psyche can no longer safely store unresolved survival data, it opens an access route. That route is the nightmare. This is not dysfunction—it is escalation toward resolution.

Most people attempt to flee nightmares because they mistake intensity for danger. In reality, intensity marks **proximity**. The closer consciousness moves to the source of fear, the stronger the sensory charge becomes. This increase is not meant to repel you; it is meant to signal that you are near something powerful and unfinished.

Avoidance teaches fear to fragment. Each time a nightmare is dismissed, the psyche breaks the fear into smaller pieces and redistributes them across waking life. This is how one dream becomes dozens of daily anxieties, money hesitations, and exhaustion loops. Engagement reverses this fragmentation.

By reframing nightmares as portals, the reader exits the victim position. The dream is no longer happening *to* them. It is opening *for* them.

Advanced Identification of Fear-Rich Dreams

At this level, fear-rich dreams are no longer obvious. They are subtle, structured, and rule-bound. These dreams behave like systems rather than stories. They contain conditions, penalties, and invisible authorities. Their purpose is not expression—it is containment.

Advanced fear-rich dreams often feel emotionally muted yet heavy. The body wakes tense even when the dream felt "quiet." This indicates compressed fear rather than explosive fear. Compression is more valuable, not less, because it contains higher potential energy.

These dreams often involve delayed consequences. Something is wrong, but punishment or loss is postponed. This trains the nervous system to live in anticipation rather than action. In wealth terms, this produces chronic waiting, hesitation, and missed timing.

Recognizing these dreams requires attention to **structure**, not imagery. Ask: Does this dream restrict movement? Does it impose rules? Does it end before resolution? If yes, it is fear-rich.

The Moment Fear Peaks Is the Doorway

Fear does not peak randomly. It peaks when the psyche has reached the maximum tolerable distance from the source of threat. At that moment, narrative collapses. Language fades. What remains is **pure perception**. This is the portal point.

Most nightmares end here because entry requires conscious consent. Without consent, the mind aborts the sequence to prevent overload. The sudden waking, the jolt, the racing heart—these are emergency exits, not failures.

The reader must learn to identify this exact instant. Not the chase. Not the tension. The *snap*—the moment fear crystallizes and time seems to stall. That instant is the threshold.

Once recognized, fear loses its ability to surprise. Surprise is what disempowers. Recognition restores orientation.

Why the Dream Always Stops at the Gate

The dream stops because the system has delivered you to the boundary of stored power. Crossing without preparation would flood the psyche. This is why repeated nightmares feel unfinished—they are unfinished by design.

Each repetition is an invitation, not a punishment. The psyche is asking: *Are you ready to enter consciously, or will you keep being ejected?*

The reader must understand that nightmares do not want resolution inside the dream state alone. They want **translation into waking authority**. This is why dream interpretation without engagement fails.

The stopping point is not denial—it is containment awaiting consent.

Lineage Imprints: Fear Older Than Choice

Some fears arrive fully formed. They do not respond to reassurance, logic, or success. These fears belong to **lineage memory**—patterns transmitted through nervous systems across generations.

Dreams are where lineage imprints surface most clearly because the waking mind no longer filters for relevance. Hunger dreams, punishment dreams, endless labor dreams—these are not personal anxieties. They are inherited survival programs still running.

The danger is misidentification. When inherited fear is treated as personal failure, shame forms. Shame locks the imprint in place. Recognition loosens it.

This chapter teaches the reader to separate **origin from ownership**.

Starvation Dreams and Famine Coding

Starvation dreams do not predict future lack. They encode **ancestral proximity to collapse**. Even if the reader has never experienced hunger, the nervous system may still carry famine logic.

These dreams create urgency without clarity. They push hoarding, overworking, under-charging, and fear of rest. Wealth cannot stabilize in a system trained to expect disappearance.

By identifying starvation imagery as lineage-based, the reader removes self-blame and prepares the fear for consumption rather than obedience.

Hoarding Imagery and Possession Anxiety

Dreams of hiding objects, clutching valuables, or losing possessions encode distrust of continuity. They assume that what exists now will vanish later.

This produces attachment without strategy—saving without investing, holding without circulating. Money becomes emotionally charged rather than functional.

Recognizing hoarding imagery as inherited allows the reader to loosen grip without triggering panic.

Authority Punishment Dreams

Authority dreams involve rules, inspections, or punishment for deviation. They encode obedience as survival.

These dreams block pricing power, boundary setting, and refusal. Even when authority figures are absent in waking life, their dream presence maintains submission.

The reader learns to identify when authority symbols belong to past generations rather than present reality.

Inescapable Labor Cycles

Dreams of endless work with no completion encode the belief that rest equals danger. These dreams produce burnout before success arrives.

They teach the system that effort never results in safety. This blocks wealth retention.

Identification is the first fracture in this loop.

Symbols That Do Not Belong to the Present Self

Some dream symbols feel subtly wrong. Foreign currencies, obsolete tools, unfamiliar customs, outdated technologies, or social rules that no longer exist. These symbols signal that the fear originates in a **non-present timeline**—a different era, culture, or survival context.

When these symbols are misinterpreted as current threats, the reader may attempt to solve problems that do not exist. Energy is wasted preparing for dangers that belong to another time. Confusion increases because solutions never quite fit.

Marking these symbols as non-present is not dismissal—it is **proper placement**. The fear is acknowledged without being obeyed. This preserves clarity and prevents misapplication of effort.

Once identified, these symbols become clear candidates for Dream-Eater engagement. They are rich in stored energy precisely because they no longer belong.

First Contact: Acknowledging the Dream-Eater

First contact is not summoning, commanding, or feeding. It is **recognition**. The Dream-Eater is acknowledged as a consuming force capable of metabolizing fear, but it is not activated yet. This distinction is critical for safety and sovereignty.

Acknowledgment establishes a new internal truth: fear does not exist without a consumer. It is no longer infinite, unmanageable, or dominant. It is something that can be processed.

No transfer occurs at this stage. The reader does not offer fear yet. They simply recognize that an alternative to obedience exists. This alone weakens fear's authority.

By delaying feeding, the system avoids overload. Power is approached gradually, with consent and structure.

Consent Before Consumption

Fear must be offered, not taken. When fear is consumed without readiness, the psyche destabilizes. This can produce dissociation, obsession, or emotional flooding. Consent ensures integration rather than fracture.

This section establishes that **control remains with the reader at all times**. Entry, feeding, and transformation occur only when readiness is present. There is no obligation to proceed simply because a portal exists.

Consent also restores dignity. Fear is no longer something that attacks or overwhelms—it is something the reader chooses to work with. Choice transforms relationship.

By ending the chapter here, the reader stands oriented, not rushed. They know the door exists. They know something can consume what they carry. And they know they decide when the exchange begins.

EXERCISE 1 — Fear-Rich Dream Re-Entry (Conscious Recall)

Purpose:
To safely re-enter a fear-rich dream without reliving or suppressing it, allowing identification of the portal point.

Step 1:
Sit upright in a quiet space during waking hours. Do not perform this exercise immediately after waking from the nightmare.

Step 2:
Close your eyes and recall the dream only up to the moment *before* fear spikes. Stop before panic, pursuit, or collapse.

Step 3:
Hold the image steady and notice physical sensations in the body. Identify where tension gathers.

Step 4:
Slow your breath until the body remains calm while the image stays present. This teaches the nervous system that fear can be observed without control.

Step 5:
Now allow the dream to move forward until fear peaks. The instant discomfort increases sharply, **stop**. That stopping point is the portal.

Step 6:
Open your eyes and write one sentence describing that exact moment.

Result:
You have located the doorway without entering it.

EXERCISE 2 — Lineage Script Identification

Purpose:

To separate inherited fear from present-life conditioning.

Step 1:

Review three fear-rich dreams from your records.

Step 2:

List the dominant themes (hunger, authority, endless work, loss).

Step 3:

Ask: *"Would this fear make sense if I lived 100 years ago?"*

Step 4:

Notice bodily response. Heaviness or familiarity indicates lineage imprint.

Step 5:

Write "Inherited" or "Present" beside each theme.

Result:

Fear loses personalization and becomes material.

EXERCISE 3 — Symbol Ownership Sorting

Purpose:

To identify dream symbols that do not belong to your current identity.

Step 1:

List all objects, currencies, tools, or social rules present in a nightmare.

Step 2:

Mark which feel outdated, unfamiliar, or historically distant.

Step 3:

Ask: *"Do I interact with this symbol in waking life?"*

Step 4:

Circle symbols that do not belong to the present self.

Step 5:

Set these aside as **non-current fear containers**.

Result:

Misplaced fear is isolated for consumption later.

SPELLS :

SPELL 1 — Portal Marking Spell

Purpose:

To mark a nightmare as an access point rather than a threat.

Timing:

Within 24 hours of a fear-rich dream.

Steps:

1. Sit with the written dream record.
2. Underline the moment fear peaked.
3. Place your finger on that line.
4. Speak aloud:
   "This moment is a doorway, not a warning."
5. Pause and breathe until the body softens.
6. Close the notebook intentionally.

Effect:

Fear stops escalating and begins organizing.

SPELL 2 — Lineage Severance Acknowledgment

Purpose:

To break automatic obedience to inherited scarcity scripts.

Steps:

1. Stand upright with feet planted.
2. Recall a lineage-coded dream theme (hunger, punishment, endless work).
3. Place one hand on the chest.
4. Speak clearly:
   "This fear is older than me. I carry it, but I do not serve it."
5. Exhale slowly through the mouth.
6. Remain still for three breaths.

Effect:

Inherited fear loosens authority without destabilization.

SPELL 3 — First Invocation: Recognition Only

Purpose:

To acknowledge the Dream-Eater without feeding or release.

Steps:

1. Sit facing an open space in the room.
2. Place one hand on the abdomen, one on the chest.
3. Speak slowly and evenly:
   **"Consumer of fear, you are recognized.
   I do not offer yet.
   I see you, and I remain sovereign."**
4. Pause for five breaths.
5. End by saying: **"Remain contained."**

Effect:

Fear is no longer alone. Power is acknowledged but restrained.

MEDITATION — Standing at the Nightmare Gate

Purpose:

To train calm presence at the portal without entry.

Steps:

1. Sit upright with spine supported.
2. Close your eyes and slow your breath until stable.
3. Recall the nightmare up to the peak-fear moment only.
4. Visualize that moment as a doorway or threshold.
5. Stand before it mentally. Do not open it.
6. Notice bodily reactions without changing them.
7. Breathe until urgency dissolves into neutrality.
8. Imagine the doorway remaining closed but visible.
9. Open your eyes gently.
10. Ground by touching a solid object nearby.

Effect:

Fear loses control while remaining accessible.

JOURNAL PROMPTS

1. Which fears in my dreams feel older than my lifetime?
2. What authority figures appear repeatedly, and do they exist now?
3. Where does hunger or deprivation appear symbolically?
4. Which dream symbols feel historically misplaced?
5. What happens at the exact moment fear peaks?
6. How does my body react before my mind does?
7. Which fears feel inherited rather than chosen?
8. What would change if fear were consumed, not obeyed?
9. How does scarcity appear when no real lack exists?
10. What am I not yet ready to offer — and why?

Closing Integration Note

At this stage, fear is no longer chaos.

It has shape.
It has history.
It has a doorway.

You are no longer trapped inside nightmares — you are standing at their threshold, aware that something exists capable of consuming what you inherited.

CHAPTER 3 — Building the Dream-Eater Shrine

Why Containment Comes Before Power

Fear does not destroy people because it is strong. It destroys people because it is **uncontained**. When fear has no place to go, it leaks—into behavior, speech, money decisions, relationships, and timing. Containment is not suppression. It is **direction**.

The Dream-Eater cannot be invoked safely without structure. Power without containment produces obsession, spirals, and identity collapse. This chapter exists to prevent that outcome. The shrine is not a place of worship. It is a **processing chamber**.

Containment creates authority. Authority allows consumption. Without authority, fear remains ambient and uncontrollable.

This chapter establishes the conditions under which fear can be **eaten instead of endured**.

The Shrine Is Internal, Not Imagined

The shrine is not a visualization exercise. It is an **internal location of function**. It exists where attention, emotion, and intention converge. You are not pretending it exists—you are assigning fear a place it must report to.

Internal structures are more stable than imagined ones because they are **felt**, not seen. The shrine becomes real through repeated use, not description.

Fear respects structure. When a container exists, fear moves toward it automatically. This is why panic subsides when boundaries are firm.

The shrine becomes the **only legal place** fear is allowed to gather.

Boundary: The Outer Wall of the Shrine

The boundary defines what fear can and cannot do. Without a boundary, fear migrates into waking life. With a boundary, fear is restricted to processing space.

The boundary is not aggressive. It is absolute. Fear is allowed inside, but nowhere else. This immediately reduces leakage.

Boundaries prevent rumination, compulsive planning, and emotional spillover. They create a **closed circuit**.

Once established, fear stops roaming. It waits.

Offering Channel: How Fear Enters

Fear must have a **pathway** into the shrine. Without a channel, fear resists containment. The offering channel is the intentional route fear follows from dream to shrine.

This channel prevents dumping. Fear is not thrown inside—it is **guided**. This preserves clarity and prevents overwhelm.

Dream imagery enters first, emotion second. This order matters. Image stabilizes emotion.

Once the channel exists, fear arrives already prepared for consumption.

Consumption Symbol: The Anchor of Metabolism

The consumption symbol is not decorative. It is the **anchor that tells the psyche fear will be used, not stored**.

Symbols work because the nervous system recognizes function before language. The symbol represents digestion, not destruction.

Fear is not annihilated—it is broken down into usable components: attention, clarity, instinct.

Without a consumption symbol, fear accumulates. With one, fear transforms.

Installing the Shrine (Internal Construction)

Installation happens gradually. Rushing creates instability. The shrine is installed through repetition, not force.

Each component is placed deliberately: boundary first, channel second, symbol last. This sequence prevents overload.

Once installed, the shrine does not require visualization. It functions automatically when fear appears.

Installation is complete when fear begins to **move on its own** toward the shrine.

Dream-to-Shrine Transfer Protocol

Nightmare imagery is transferred, not relived. Reliving feeds fear. Transfer feeds the Dream-Eater.

Images are brought in stripped of narrative. Only the core remains. This prevents emotional flooding.

Transfer is brief, precise, and closed. Fear is not invited to linger.

Over time, nightmares shorten. Fear learns there is a faster route to consumption.

Metabolizing Emotional Charge

Emotion is energy without direction. The shrine provides direction. Emotional charge is broken down into **focus and readiness**.

Metabolism happens automatically once the shrine is active. You do not force calm—you allow digestion.

This prevents panic loops and emotional hangovers.

Fear leaves behind **clarity instead of residue**.

Energy Redirection Rule One: Fear Becomes Focus

Fear sharpens perception. When redirected, it becomes focus. This is the first conversion.

Instead of scattering attention, fear now concentrates it. Decisions become precise rather than rushed.

Focus replaces urgency. Action becomes intentional.

This rule stabilizes money decisions immediately.

Energy Redirection Rule Two: Panic Becomes Precision

Panic is fear without containment. Precision is fear with structure.

Once panic enters the shrine, it is reduced to actionable data. What matters becomes obvious. What does not falls away.

This ends overreaction and undercharging.

Precision restores timing.

The Dream-Eater as Internal Consumer

The Dream-Eater is not an external being. It is a **consuming function** within the shrine.

It does not judge fear. It consumes it. Judgment preserves fear. Consumption dissolves it.

Acknowledgment activates the function. Feeding comes later.

For now, the Dream-Eater waits inside structure.

Stability Before Feeding

This chapter ends without feeding for a reason. Stability must precede power.

Fear now has a place. A path. A consumer. Nothing is leaking.

Only when fear stays contained consistently is feeding introduced.

EXERCISES:

Exercise 1 — Boundary Installation

Step 1: Sit quietly and locate where fear gathers in your body.

Step 2: Imagine a firm perimeter around that space.

Step 3: Say internally: *"Fear belongs here, nowhere else."*

Step 4: Notice reduction in background anxiety.

Step 5: Repeat nightly for five days.

Exercise 2 — Offering Channel Activation

Step 1: Recall a fear-rich dream image.

Step 2: Guide it mentally into the shrine space.

Step 3: Do not analyze.

Step 4: Close the channel immediately after entry.

Step 5: Ground physically.

Exercise 3 — Leakage Detection

Step 1: Notice fear appearing during the day.

Step 2: Ask: *"Did this go to the shrine?"*

Step 3: If not, redirect it immediately.

Step 4: Observe stabilization.

SPELLS:

Spell 1 — Shrine Establishment Spell
Steps:

1. Sit upright.
2. Place hand on chest.
3. Speak:
   “Fear has a place.
   It does not wander.”
4. Breathe until calm.
5. End deliberately.

Spell 2 — Containment Seal
Steps:

1. Recall fear briefly.
2. Direct it inward.
3. Say:
   **"Contained.
   Await consumption."**
4. Pause three breaths.

Spell 3 — Consumer Acknowledgment
Steps:

1. Sit facing open space.
2. Say:
   "Dream-Eater, remain within structure."
3. Feel stability.
4. Close.

MEDITATION — Activating the Shrine
Steps:

1. Sit upright, eyes closed.
2. Breathe until steady.
3. Sense the shrine's boundary.
4. Sense the offering channel.
5. Sense the consumption symbol.
6. Feel fear move inward.
7. Remain until calm.
8. End intentionally.

JOURNAL PROMPTS

1. Where did fear roam before containment?
2. How does my body respond to structure?
3. What changes when fear has a place?
4. Where does panic lose power?
5. How does focus feel different from urgency?
6. What stabilizes first—emotion or thought?
7. How does money fear change?
8. What no longer leaks?
9. When does fear become useful?
10. What feels safer now?

Closing Reflection

Fear is no longer ambient.
It no longer whispers into every decision.
It no longer drains you invisibly.

Fear now has a place.
A path.
A consumer.

You are no longer managing fear—you are **containing it.**
The Dream-Eater will not just wait.

It will begin to eat.

CHAPTER 4 — Lucid Wealth Incantations

Why Conversion Must Happen Between States

Fear is most powerful at the border between sleep and waking. In full waking consciousness, the mind defends its habits. In deep sleep, the mind is too diffuse to program. The hypnagogic state—the drifting threshold between—temporarily **disables resistance** while keeping intention intact.

This is where wealth conditioning must occur. Not through affirmations repeated during the day, but through **incantations spoken when the scarcity generator is offline**. At this threshold, fear has surfaced but has not yet hardened into behavior.

This chapter teaches how to use that moment deliberately. Conversion happens before fear can become urgency, avoidance, or contraction.

Once conversion is learned, scarcity never fully forms.

Hypnagogia: The Wealth Programming Window

Hypnagogia is the moment when thought becomes fluid but meaning remains precise. Sensations drift. Images flicker. Language loosens. This is not imagination—it is **neural plasticity**.

In this state, the nervous system is receptive. Scripts can be overwritten without confrontation. Fear does not argue. It listens.

The reader learns to recognize hypnagogia not by visuals, but by **felt disorientation with retained awareness**. This is the programming window.

Miss this window and fear hardens. Catch it, and fear transforms before identity reacts.

Why Incantations Work When Logic Fails

Logic negotiates with fear. Incantations **command structure**. They do not persuade—they assign function.

An incantation spoken in hypnagogia bypasses rational filtering and installs instruction directly into pattern formation. This is why incantations must be precise, short, and spoken aloud.

The voice anchors the instruction in the body. Thought alone is insufficient.

This chapter replaces passive affirmation with **directive speech**.

Scarcity Origin Points

Scarcity does not begin with money. It begins with a **micro-moment**: a sensation, a hesitation, a tightening, a rush.

That moment—when fear converts into behavior—is the scarcity origin point. Miss it, and the loop runs automatically.

The reader is taught to identify these points by sensation, not thought. Tight chest. Shallow breath. Sudden urgency. Delay.

Once identified, these points become interception zones.

Fear as a Timing Signal, Not a Warning

Fear has been misclassified as danger. In truth, fear is a **timing signal**. It appears when attention sharpens.

When fear is redirected, it no longer predicts failure—it predicts **importance**. Something requires presence.

This reframing is essential. Without it, fear always triggers avoidance or panic. With it, fear becomes a cue for precision.

This is how fear becomes advantage.

Replacing Urgency with Authority

Urgency collapses options. Authority expands them.

Urgency says *act now or lose*. Authority says *wait until alignment is exact*. Hypnagogic incantations reassign this rule at the nervous system level.

Once urgency is replaced, decisions slow just enough to become accurate. Money stops leaking through rushed action.

This shift alone produces measurable change.

Converting Fear Into Timing

Fear sharpens awareness. Timing uses that awareness strategically.

This section teaches the reader to **pause inside fear**, not escape it. That pause creates temporal leverage.

In hypnagogia, timing scripts can be installed so fear triggers patience instead of reaction.

This ends impulsive spending, underpricing, and premature commitment.

Anchoring Abundance Into the Nervous System

Abundance must be felt as safe or it will be rejected. The nervous system—not belief—decides safety.

Incantations spoken in hypnagogia anchor abundance as **neutral and expected**, not threatening or temporary.

This prevents self-sabotage after success.

Lucid Redirection in Waking Life

Once installed, incantations activate automatically. Fear arises—and instead of spiraling, it redirects.

The reader experiences this as a subtle internal shift: urgency dissolves, clarity sharpens, action becomes obvious.

This is lucid redirection. No effort. No struggle.

Fear becomes a signal, not a storm.

Why Scarcity Can Be Intercepted

Scarcity relies on speed. Interception relies on awareness.

By slowing the conversion moment by even a second, the entire loop collapses.

This chapter teaches the reader to **live inside that second**.

Stability of the Converted System

Once fear converts cleanly several times, the system stabilizes. Scarcity loses credibility.

The reader no longer reacts automatically. Choice returns.

This is the beginning of financial invincibility.

Preparation for Feeding

Conversion prepares the ground for Chapter 5. Fear is no longer chaotic. It is usable.

The Dream-Eater will soon be fed directly—but only after programming is stable.

EXERCISES:

Exercise 1 — Hypnagogic Detection

Step 1: Lie down at night with lights off.

Step 2: Keep eyes closed and observe drifting thoughts.

Step 3: Notice when thoughts lose linear structure.

Step 4: Confirm awareness is still present.

Step 5: This is the programming window.

Exercise 2 — Scarcity Origin Tracking

Step 1: Notice fear during a money decision.

Step 2: Freeze for three seconds.

Step 3: Identify first bodily sensation.

Step 4: Record it later.

Step 5: This is your origin point.

Exercise 3 — Authority Installation

Step 1: Recall urgency.

Step 2: Pause inside it.

Step 3: Breathe until calm.

Step 4: Say internally: *"I decide when."*

Step 5: Act only after clarity.

SPELLS:

Spell 1 — Urgency Dissolution Incantation
Timing: Hypnagogic state.
Steps:

1. Allow body to soften.
2. Speak aloud:
   **"Urgency dissolves.
   Authority remains."**
3. Repeat once.
4. Sleep.

Spell 2 — Fear-to-Timing Conversion
Steps:

1. Recall a fear sensation.
2. Pause.
3. Speak:
   "This fear sharpens timing."
4. Breathe until settled.

Spell 3 — Abundance Anchoring
Steps:

1. Enter hypnagogia.
2. Say:
   “Abundance is stable.
   I remain safe.”
3. Let sleep take over.

MEDITATION — Lucid Wealth Threshold
Steps:

1. Sit or lie comfortably.
2. Breathe until slow.
3. Recall a fear moment.
4. Do not judge it.
5. Feel clarity emerge.
6. Name the right action mentally.
7. Let sensation settle.
8. End without force.

JOURNAL PROMPTS

1. When does fear first appear?
2. What does urgency feel like physically?
3. How does authority feel different?
4. Where have I rushed before?
5. What changes when I pause?
6. How does fear sharpen clarity?
7. What timing feels correct now?
8. Where does abundance feel unsafe?
9. How does my body respond to calm?
10. What no longer controls me?

Closing Reflection

Scarcity no longer forms automatically.
You have learned to intercept it at birth.

Fear no longer rushes you.
It informs you.

Urgency no longer commands you.
Authority replaces it.

You are no longer reacting to money.
You are **programming the moment it would have ruled you**.

CHAPTER 5 — Your Fortune Feeding Cycle

Why Power Must Become Cyclical

Power that requires constant effort collapses. Power that feeds itself stabilizes. The purpose of this chapter is to end dependency on rituals, moods, or heightened states and replace them with a **closed-loop system**. Once installed, the Fortune Feeding Cycle runs automatically, responding to fear as fuel rather than threat.

Most systems fail because they require vigilance. This one succeeds because it **uses what already appears**. Fear will arise whether invited or not. This chapter ensures fear no longer disrupts—it supplies.

Autonomy is achieved when the system continues without conscious forcing. Continuity is achieved when it continues without degeneration.

This chapter completes that transition.

Fear as Renewable Fuel, Not an Emergency

Fear does not need to be eliminated to lose power. It needs to be **reclassified**. When fear is treated as danger, the body reacts. When fear is treated as fuel, the body stabilizes.

Renewable fear differs from panic. Panic is fear without structure. Fuel is fear with destination. The Fortune Feeding Cycle gives fear a destination every time it appears.

This reclassification ends emotional volatility. Fear becomes predictable. Predictability creates calm.

From this point forward, fear is no longer disruptive—it is **expected input**.

The Fortune Feeding Loop Explained

The loop functions because each stage prepares the next. Remove one, and the system destabilizes. Together, they create continuity.

1. **Fear appears** — inevitable, neutral, informational
2. **Dream captures it** — fear is collected during sleep, not carried into the day
3. **Dream-Eater consumes it** — fear is metabolized, not stored
4. **Waking action gains clarity** — behavior sharpens instead of contracts
5. **Wealth behavior stabilizes** — decisions become consistent, not reactive

The loop closes by turning outcome into confidence, which reduces baseline fear intensity over time.

This is how scarcity ends **without suppression**.

Tracking Fear Without Obsession

Tracking does not mean monitoring constantly. It means **recognizing patterns without fixation**. The system does the work; awareness confirms it.

The reader is taught to notice only three things:

- When fear appears
- Where it goes
- What clarity follows

No analysis. No journaling every instance. Obsession starves the system by over-interfering.

Minimal awareness preserves autonomy.

How Dreams Capture Fear Automatically

Once the shrine and incantations are active, dreams take over fear collection. This prevents daytime rumination and nighttime escalation.

Fear that appears during the day no longer seeks resolution immediately. It waits. The psyche knows where it will be processed.

This alone eliminates urgency-driven behavior.

Dreams become functional rather than chaotic. Nightmares shorten. Symbolism simplifies.

Fear learns the system works.

The Dream-Eater's Role in Long-Term Stability

The Dream-Eater no longer requires invocation once the cycle is active. It operates as a **background metabolic function**.

Consumption happens quietly. Fear is broken down into focus, timing, and decisiveness.

No emotional high follows. No crash occurs. Stability replaces intensity.

This is how power becomes sustainable.

Waking Action as Proof of Consumption

The only reliable sign that fear has been consumed is **clarity in action**. Decisions become slower but sharper. Impulses fade. Boundaries hold.

Money behavior stabilizes because it is no longer driven by urgency, shame, or anticipation of loss.

This is not discipline—it is **alignment**.

Final Severance of Inherited Poverty Patterns

Inherited patterns persist until they are consciously released. This chapter performs the final severance—not through denial, but through **closure**.

Once fear stops returning as scarcity behavior, lineage scripts lose relevance. They no longer find traction.

Severance is not rebellion against ancestors. It is **completion of their unfinished survival work**.

This reframes release as respect.

Inherited Pattern Severance Ritual (Core Working)

RITUAL — The Lineage Closure Rite

Purpose:

To formally end obedience to inherited scarcity patterns.

Steps:

1. Sit quietly at night before sleep.
2. Name aloud one recurring fear that feels inherited.
3. Say clearly:
   **"This fear kept others alive.
   It no longer governs me."**
4. Place one hand on the chest.
5. Breathe until the body softens.
6. End without elaboration.

Effect:

The pattern loses authority without resistance.

Long-Term Maintenance Rules

The system requires only three rules:

1. **Do not chase fear.** Let it appear naturally.
2. **Do not suppress fear.** Suppression restarts leakage.
3. **Do not dramatize fear.** Drama feeds identity loops.

Follow these rules and the cycle maintains itself.

Breaking them temporarily does not collapse the system—it only slows it.

Preventing Relapse into Scarcity Identity

Relapse happens when identity reattaches to fear. The reader is taught to watch for identity statements such as *"I always struggle"* or *"Money is hard."*

These statements are not truths—they are echoes.

When noticed, no correction is required. The system already handles the fear. Identity follows behavior, not belief.

As wealth behavior stabilizes, identity updates automatically.

When Fear Returns as Power Supply

Eventually, fear stops feeling personal. It arrives with information instead of threat.

Fear becomes the signal that something important is forming—an opportunity, a decision, a transition.

At this stage, fear no longer precedes collapse. It precedes **expansion**.

This is the final transformation.

EXERCISES:

Exercise 1 — Loop Confirmation

Step 1: Notice fear during the day.

Step 2: Do nothing with it.

Step 3: Observe clarity the following day.

Step 4: Record the change.

Step 5: Trust the system.

Exercise 2 — Behavior Stabilization Check

Step 1: Review one financial decision weekly.

Step 2: Note emotional tone.

Step 3: Compare to previous months.

Step 4: Identify increased calm.

Step 5: Reinforce consistency.

Exercise 3 — Identity Release

Step 1: Catch a scarcity self-statement.

Step 2: Pause.

Step 3: Ask: *"Is this current?"*

Step 4: Do not answer.

Step 5: Move on.

SPELLS:

Spell 1 — Cycle Lock Spell
Steps:

1. Sit upright.
2. Say:
   "Fear feeds clarity.
   Clarity feeds wealth."
3. Breathe three times.
4. End deliberately.

Spell 2 — Scarcity Relapse Seal
Steps:

1. Place hand on chest.
2. Say:
   “I do not return.”
3. Pause.
4. Continue day.

Spell 3 — Power Return Invocation
Steps:

1. Notice fear.
2. Say internally:
   "Fuel received."
3. Act later from clarity.

MEDITATION — The Closed Circuit
Steps:

1. Sit comfortably.
2. Breathe until calm.
3. Recall a fear that once caused scarcity.
4. Observe neutrality now.
5. Feel stability in the body.
6. Let the loop complete itself.
7. End without force.

JOURNAL PROMPTS

1. How does fear feel different now?
2. What behaviors have stabilized?
3. Where does urgency no longer appear?
4. What clarity follows fear?
5. Which inherited fears feel complete?
6. How does money feel emotionally?
7. What decisions feel easier?
8. What no longer defines me?
9. How does rest feel now?
10. What power now feeds me?

Closing Reflection

Fear no longer chases you.
It no longer warns you.
It no longer controls you.

Fear now **feeds** you.

What once drained your future now powers it.
What once repeated now completes.
What once haunted now supplies strength.

The cycle is closed.
The system runs.
Your fortune is no longer defended—it is **fed**.

This is autonomy.
This is continuity.
This is invincibility.

APPENDIX A — Dream Invocation Charts for Wealth Convergence

Purpose of This Appendix

This appendix exists to **remove guesswork** from dream-based wealth work.
Dreams become chaotic when treated symbolically. They become powerful when treated **procedurally**.

The Dream Invocation Charts provide:

- A **clear mapping** between dream states and wealth outcomes
- Exact **invocation timing windows**
- Specific **actions to take or avoid** after each dream category
- A way to **converge fear, clarity, and money behavior** into a single operating system

These charts are not predictive.
They are **convergent**—they bring scattered signals into alignment.

How to Use the Charts (Before You Begin)

1. Do not use all charts at once
2. Identify the chart that matches the dream *state*, not the dream story
3. Apply the invocation within **24 hours** of the dream
4. Take one aligned waking action only
5. Allow the system to stabilize

Overuse fragments results.
Precision compounds them.

CHART 1 — Fear Density to Wealth Signal Conversion

Use When:

A dream produces lingering unease, urgency, or pressure without clear narrative meaning.

Dream Indicators

- Emotional heaviness upon waking
- Repeating locations
- Sudden interruption at peak fear
- No clear resolution

Invocation Window

- Immediately upon waking
- Or during hypnagogia the following night

Invocation Phrase

"This fear sharpens clarity.
Clarity directs wealth."

Wealth Convergence Action

- Delay all money decisions for 24 hours
- Observe which option remains calm

Result

Fear converts into **timing awareness**, preventing rushed loss.

CHART 2 — Starvation & Lack Dreams → Abundance Stabilization

Use When:

Dreams include hunger, empty stores, rationing, or denied access to resources.

Dream Indicators

- Food present but unreachable
- Empty shelves
- Waiting endlessly for supply

Invocation Window

- Morning stillness before speaking to anyone

Invocation Phrase

"Access is stable.
I am not late."

Wealth Convergence Action

- Spend or invest a **small, intentional amount** the same day
- Do not hoard

Result

Breaks famine reflex and restores **circulation trust**.

CHART 3 — Hoarding Dreams → Circulation Reprogramming

Use When:

Dreams involve hiding valuables, locking doors, losing possessions, or obsessive protection.

Dream Indicators

- Anxiety about loss without visible threat
- Clutching objects
- Panic over missing items

Invocation Window

- Before sleep the following night

Invocation Phrase

"What moves returns multiplied.
What stagnates decays."

Wealth Convergence Action

- Release something financial or material voluntarily
- Cancel, donate, upgrade, or invest

Result

Restores **flow dominance** over attachment.

CHART 4 — Authority & Punishment Dreams → Sovereignty Activation

Use When:

Dreams include inspectors, supervisors, judges, rules, or punishment for deviation.

Dream Indicators

- Fear of doing something "wrong"
- Unclear rules
- Punishment without explanation

Invocation Window

- Standing position during waking hours

Invocation Phrase

"No authority governs my value.
I self-authorize."

Wealth Convergence Action

- Raise a price, set a boundary, or say no once
- Even minimally

Result

Restores **pricing power and self-permission**.

CHART 5 — Endless Labor Dreams → Completion Encoding

Use When:

Dreams involve nonstop work, unfinished tasks, or progress that resets.

Dream Indicators

- No reward
- No endpoint
- Repetition

Invocation Window

- Midday pause

Invocation Phrase

"Effort concludes.
Safety follows completion."

Wealth Convergence Action

- Finish one task completely and stop
- Do not start another immediately

Result

Retrains nervous system to associate **completion with safety**, not danger.

CHART 6 — Peak-Fear Interruption Dreams → Opportunity Mapping

Use When:

Dream ends abruptly at maximum fear or intensity.

Dream Indicators

- Sudden awakening
- Shock or jolt
- No resolution

Invocation Window

- Within 10 minutes of waking

Invocation Phrase

"The interruption marks advantage.
I will see it."

Wealth Convergence Action

- Watch for unexpected opportunity within 72 hours
- Act calmly, not eagerly

Result

Fear becomes **early-warning intelligence**, not threat.

CHART 7 — Obscure or Outdated Symbols → Lineage Release

Use When:

Dream includes old currencies, tools, customs, or unfamiliar environments.

Dream Indicators

- Historical feel
- Foreign systems
- Symbols that don't belong to your life

Invocation Window

- Night before sleep

Invocation Phrase

"This fear is complete.
Its task is finished."

Wealth Convergence Action

- Do nothing for 24 hours
- Allow nervous system recalibration

Result

Closes inherited loops without conflict.

CHART 8 — Repeating Nightmares → Consumption Acceleration

Use When:

The same dream or theme repeats over multiple nights.

Dream Indicators

- Identical fear patterns
- Same location or threat

Invocation Window

- Shrine meditation session

Invocation Phrase

"This is ready.
Consume fully."

Wealth Convergence Action

- Take one decisive money-related action within 48 hours
- No overthinking

Result

Prevents recurrence and **releases stored charge**.

CHART 9 — Calm Dreams After Fear → Integration Phase
Use When:
Fear has recently diminished and dreams feel neutral or quiet.
Dream Indicators

- Reduced intensity
- Absence of threat

Invocation Window

- Optional; not required

Invocation Phrase
"Integration complete."
Wealth Convergence Action

- Maintain routine
- Avoid unnecessary rituals

Result
System stabilizes; do not disrupt.

CHART 10 — No Dreams Remembered → System Trust Mode

Use When:

Dream recall temporarily disappears.

Dream Indicators

- Blank sleep
- No imagery

Invocation Window

- None

Invocation Phrase

None required

Wealth Convergence Action

- Continue normal behavior
- Do not force recall

Result

Indicates **successful background processing**.

Common Errors to Avoid

- Forcing interpretation
- Over-invoking multiple charts
- Chasing fear instead of waiting
- Turning charts into superstition
- Using charts to avoid real action

These charts **guide convergence**, not escape.

Closing Note

These charts do not control your dreams.
They **align what dreams already deliver**.

When used correctly:

- Fear arrives already formatted
- Dreams self-organize
- Wealth behavior stabilizes
- Scarcity loses access

You no longer wait for signs.
You **converge signals into power**.

This appendix is not optional reference.
It is the **maintenance spine** of the entire system.

Return to it when fear changes form—
not when you feel lost.

Message from the Author:

I hope you enjoyed this book, I love astrology and knew there was not a book such as this out on the shelf. I love metaphysical items as well. Please check out my other books:

-Life of Government Benefits

-My life of Hell

-My life with Hydrocephalus

-Red Sky

-World Domination:Woman's rule

-World Domination:Woman's Rule 2: The War

-Life and Banishment of Apophis: book 1

-The Kidney Friendly Diet

-The Ultimate Hemp Cookbook

-Creating a Dispensary(legally)

-Cleanliness throughout life: the importance of showering from childhood to adulthood.

-Strong Roots: The Risks of Overcoddling children

-Hemp Horoscopes: Cosmic Insights and Earthly Healing

- Celestial Hemp Navigating the Zodiac: Through the Green Cosmos

-Astrological Hemp: Aligning The Stars with Earth's Ancient Herb

-The Astrological Guide to Hemp: Stars, Signs, and Sacred Leaves

-Green Growth: Innovative Marketing Strategies for your Hemp Products and Dispensary

-Cosmic Cannabis

-Astrological Munchies

-Henry The Hemp

-Zodiacal Roots: The Astrological Soul Of Hemp

- **Green Constellations: Intersection of Hemp and Zodiac**

-Hemp in The Houses: An astrological Adventure Through The Cannabis Galaxy

-Galactic Ganja Guide

Heavenly Hemp

Zodiac Leaves

Doctor Who Astrology

Cannastrology

Stellar Satvias and Cosmic Indicas

Celestial Cannabis: A Zodiac Journey

AstroHerbology: The Sky and The Soil: Volume 1

AstroHerbology:Celestial Cannabis:Volume 2

Cosmic Cannabis Cultivation

The Starry Guide to Herbal Harmony: Volume 1

The Starry Guide to Herbal Harmony: Cannabis Universe: Volume 2

Yugioh Astrology: Astrological Guide to Deck, Duels and more

Nightmare Mansion: Echoes of The Abyss

Nightmare Mansion 2: Legacy of Shadows

Nightmare Mansion 3: Shadows of the Forgotten

Nightmare Mansion 4: Echoes of the Damned

The Life and Banishment of Apophis: Book 2

Nightmare Mansion: Halls of Despair

Healing with Herb: Cannabis and Hydrocephalus

Planetary Pot: Aligning with Astrological Herbs: Volume 1

Fast Track to Freedom: 30 Days to Financial Independence Using AI, Assets, and Agile Hustles

Cosmic Hemp Pathways

How to Become Financially Free in 30 Days: 10,000 Paths to Prosperity

Zodiacal Herbage: Astrological Insights: Volume 1

Nightmare Mansion: Whispers in the Walls

The Daleks Invade Atlantis

Henry the hemp and Hydrocephalus

10X The Kidney Friendly Diet

Cannabis Universe: Adult coloring book

Hemp Astrology: The Healing Power of the Stars

Zodiacal Herbage: Astrological Insights: Cannabis Universe: Volume 2

Planetary Pot: Aligning with Astrological Herbs: Cannabis Universes: Volume 2

Doctor Who: Convergence Protocol – The Replicator War

Nightmare Mansion: Curse of the Blood Moon

The Celestial Stoner: A Guide to the Zodiac

Cosmic Pleasures: Sex Toy Astrology for Every Sign

Hydrocephalus Astrology: Navigating the Stars and Healing Waters

Lapis and the Mischievous Chocolate Bar

Celestial Positions: Sexual Astrology for Every Sign

Apophis's Shadow Work Journal: **:** A Journey of Self-Discovery and Healing

Kinky Cosmos: Sexual Kink Astrology for Every Sign

Digital Cosmos: The Astrological Digimon Compendium

Stellar Seeds: The Cosmic Guide to Growing with Astrology

Apophis's Daily Gratitude Journal

Cat Astrology: Feline Mysteries of the Cosmos

The Cosmic Kama Sutra: An Astrological Guide to Sexual Positions

Unleash Your Potential: A Guided Journal Powered by AI Insights

Whispers of the Enchanted Grove

Cosmic Pleasures: An Astrological Guide to Sexual Kinks

369, 12 Manifestation Journal

Whisper of the nocturne journal(blank journal for writing or drawing)

The Boogey Book

Locked In Reflection: A Chastity Journey Through Locktober

Generating Wealth Quickly:How to Generate $100,000 in 24 Hours

Star Magic: Harness the Power of the Universe

The Flatulence Chronicles: A Fart Journal for Self-Discovery

The Doctor and The Death Moth

Seize the Day: A Personal Seizure Tracking Journal

The Ultimate Boogeyman Safari: A Journey into the Boogie World and Beyond

Whispers of Samhain: 1,000 Spells of Love, Luck, and Lunar Magic: Samhain Spell Book

Apophis's guides:Witch's Spellbook Crafting Guide for Halloween

Frost & Flame: The Enchanted Yule Grimoire of 1000 Winter Spells

The Ultimate Boogey Goo Guide & Spooky Activities for Halloween Fun

Harmony of the Scales: A Libra's Spellcraft for Balance and Beauty

The Enchanted Advent: 36 Days of Christmas Wonders

Nightmare Mansion: The Labyrinth of Screams

Harvest of Enchantment: 1,000 Spells of Gratitude, Love, and Fortune for Thanksgiving

The Boogey Chronicles: A Journal of Nightly Encounters and Shadowy Secrets

The 12 Days of Financial Freedom: A Step-by-Step Christmas Countdown to Transform Your Finances

Sigil of the Eternal Spiral Blank Journal

A Christmas Feast: Timeless Recipes for Every Meal

Holiday Stress-Free Solutions: A Survival Guide to Thriving During the Festive Season

Yu-Gi-Oh! Holiday Gifting Mastery: The Ultimate Guide for Fans and Newcomers Alike

Holiday Harmony: A Hydrocephalus Survival Guide for the Festive Season

Celestial Craft: The Witch's Almanac for 2025 – A Cosmic Guide to Manifestations, Moons, and Mystical Events

Doctor Who: The Toymaker's Winter Wonderland

Tulsa King Unveiled: A Thrilling Guide to Stallone's Mafia Masterpiece

Pendulum Craft: A Complete Guide to Crafting and Using Personalized Divination Tools

Nightmare Mansion: Santa's Eternal Eve

Starlight Noel: A Cosmic Journey through Christmas Mysteries

The Dark Architect: Unlocking the Blueprint of Existence

Surviving the Embrace: The Ultimate Guide to Encounters with The Hugging Molly

The Enchanted Codex: Secrets of the Craft for Witches, Wiccans, and Pagans

Harvest of Gratitude: A Complete Thanksgiving Guide

Yuletide Essentials: A Complete Guide to an Authentic and Magical Christmas

Celestial Smokes: A Cosmic Guide to Cigars and Astrology

Living in Balance: A Comprehensive Survival Guide to Thriving with Diabetes Insipidus

Cosmic Symbiosis: The Venom Zodiac Chronicles

The Cursed Paw of Ambition

Cosmic Symbiosis: The Astrological Venom Journal

Celestial Wonders Unfold: A Stargazer's Guide to the Cosmos (2024-2029)

The Ultimate Black Friday Prepper's Guide: Mastering Shopping Strategies and Savings

Cosmic Sales: The Astrological Guide to Black Friday Shopping

Legends of the Corn Mother and Other Harvest Myths

Whispers of the Harvest: The Corn Mother's Journal
The Evergreen Spellbook
The Doctor Meets the Boogeyman
The White Witch of Rose Hall's SpellBook
The Gingerbread Golem's Shadow: A Study in Sweet Darkness
The Gingerbread Golem Codex: An Academic Exploration of Sweet Myths
The Gingerbread Golem Grimoire: Sweet Magicks and Spells for the Festive Witch
The Curse of the Gingerbread Golem
10-minute Christmas Crafts for kids
Christmas Crisis Solutions: The Ultimate Last-Minute Survival Guide
Gingerbread Golem Recipes: Holiday Treats with a Magical Twist
The Infinite Key: Unlocking Mystical Secrets of the Ages
Enchanted Yule: A Wiccan and Pagan Guide to a Magical and Memorable Season
Dinosaurs of Power: Unlocking Ancient Magick
Astro-Dinos: The Cosmic Guide to Prehistoric Wisdom
Gallifrey's Yule Logs: A Festive Doctor Who Cookbook
The Dino Grimoire: Secrets of Prehistoric Magick
The Gift They Never Knew They Needed
The Gingerbread Golem's Culinary Alchemy: Enchanting Recipes for a Sweetly Dark Feast
A Time Lord Christmas: Holiday Adventures with the Doctor
Krampusproofing Your Home: Defensive Strategies for Yule
Silent Frights: A Collection of Christmas Creepypastas to Chill Your Bones
Santa Raptor's Jolly Carnage: A Dino-Claus Christmas Tale
Prehistoric Palettes: A Dino Wicca Coloring Journey
The Christmas Wishkeeper Chronicles
The Starlight Sleigh: A Holiday Journey
Elf Secrets: The True Magic of the North Pole

Candy Cane Conjurations
Cooking with Kids: Recipes Under 20 Minutes
Doctor Who: The TARDIS Confiscation
The Anxiety First Aid Kit: Quick Tools to Calm Your Mind
Frosty Whispers: A Winter's Tale
The Infinite Key: Unlocking the Secrets to Prosperity, Resilience, and Purpose
The Grasping Void: Why You'll Regret This Purchase
Astrology for Busy Bees: Star Signs Simplified
The Instant Focus Formula: Cut Through the Noise
The Secret Language of Colors: Unlocking the Emotional Codes
Sacred Fossil Chronicles: Blank Journal
The Christmas Cottage Miracle
Feeding Frenzy: Graboid-Inspired Recipes
Manifest in Minutes: The Quick Law of Attraction Guide
The Symbiote Chronicles: Doctor Who's Venomous Journey
Think Tiny, Grow Big: The Minimalist Mindset
The Energy Key: Unlocking Limitless Motivation
New Year, New Magic: Manifesting Your Best Year Yet
Unstoppable You: Mastering Confidence in Minutes
Infinite Energy: The Secret to Never Feeling Drained
Lightning Focus: Mastering the Art of Productivity in a Distracted World
Saturnalia Manifestation Magick: A Guide to Unlocking Abundance During the Solstice
Graboids and Garland: The Ultimate Tremors-Themed Christmas Guide
12 Nights of Holiday Magic
The Power of Pause: 60-Second Mindfulness Practices
The Quick Reset: How to Reclaim Your Life After Burnout
The Shadow Eater: A Tale of Despair and Survival
The Micro-Mastery Method: Transform Your Skills in Just Minutes a Day

Reclaiming Time: How to Live More by Doing Less
Chronovore: The Eternal Nexus
The Mind Reset: Unlocking Your Inner Peace in a Chaotic World
Confidence Code: Building Unshakable Self-Belief
Baby the Vampire Terrier
Baby the Vampire Terrier's Christmas Adventure
Celestial Streams: The Content Creator's Astrology Manual
The Wealth Whisperer: Unlocking Abundance with Everyday Actions
The Energy Equation: Maximize Your Output Without Burning Out
The Happiness Algorithm: Science-Backed Steps to Joyful Living
Stress-Free Success: Achieving Goals Without Anxiety
Mindful Wealth: The New Blueprint for Financial Freedom
The Festive Flavors of New Year: A Culinary Celebration
The Master's Gambit: Keys of Eternal Power
Shadowed Secrets: Groundhog Day Mysteries
Beneath the Burrow: Lessons from the Groundhog
Spring's Whispers: The Groundhog's Prediction
The Limitless Mindset: Unlock Your Untapped Potential
The Focus Funnel: How to Cut Through Chaos and Get Results
Bold Moves: Building Courage to Live on Your Terms
The Daily Shift: Simple Practices for Lasting Transformation
The Quarter-Life Reset: Thriving in Your 20s and 30s
The Art of Shadowplay: Building Your Own Personal Myth
The Eternal Loop: Finding Purpose in Repetition
Burrowing Wisdom: Life Lessons from the Groundhog
Shadow Work: A Groundhog Day Perspective
Love in Bloom: 5-Minute Romantic Gestures
The Shadowspell Codex: Secrets of Forbidden Magick
The Burnout Cure: Finding Balance in a Busy World
The Groundhog Prophecy: Unlocking Seasonal Secrets
Nog Tales: The Spirited History of Eggnog

Six More Weeks: Embracing Seasonal Transitions
The Lumivian Chronicles: Fragments of the Fifth Dimension
Money on Your Mind: A Beginner's Guide to Wealth
The Focus Fix: Breaking Through Distraction
January's Spirit Keepers: Mystical Protectors of the Cold
Creativity Unchained: Unlocking Your Wildest Ideas in 2025
Manifestation Mastery: 365 Days to Rewrite Your Reality
The Groundhog's Mirror: Reflecting on Change
The Weeping Angels' Christmas Curse
Burrowed in Time: A Groundhog Day Journey
Heartbeats: Poems to Share with Your Valentine
Dino Wicca: The Sacred Grimoire of Prehistoric Magick
Courage of the Pride: Finding Your Inner Roar
The Lion's Leap: Bold Moves for Big Results
Healthy Hustle: Achieving Without Overworking
Practical Manifesting: Turning Dreams into Reality in 2025
Jurassic Pharaohs: Unlocking the Magick of Ancient Egypt and Dino Wicca
The Happiness Equation: Small Changes for Big Joy
The Confidence Compass: Finding Your Inner Strength
Whispers in the Hollow: Tales of the Forgotten Beasts
Echoes from the Hollow: The Return of Forgotten Beasts
The Hollow Ascendant: The Rise of the Forgotten Beasts
The Relationship Reset: Building Better Connections
Mastering the Morning: How to Win the Day Before 8 AM
The Shadow's Dance: Groundhog Day Symbolism
Cupid's Kitchen: Quick Valentine's Day Recipes
Valentine's Day on a Budget: Love Without Breaking the Bank
Astrocraft: Aligning the Stars in the World of Minecraft
Forecasting Life: Groundhog Day Reflections
Bleeding Hearts: Twisted Tales of Valentine's Terror
Herbal Smoke Revolution: The Ultimate Guide to Nature's Cigarette Alternative

Winter's Wrath: The Complete Survival Blueprint for Extreme Freezes.

The Groundhog's Shadow: A Tale of Seasons

Burrowed Insights: Wisdom from the Groundhog

Sensual Strings: The Art of Erotic Bondage

Whispered Flames: Unlocking the Power of Fire Play

Forgotten Shadows: A Guide to Cryptids Lost to Time

Six Weeks of Secrets: Groundhog Day's Hidden Messages

Shadows and Cycles: Groundhog Day Reflections

The Art of Love Letters: Crafting the Perfect Message

Romantic Getaways at Home: Turning Your Space into Paradise

Purrfect Brews: A Cat Lover's Guide to Coffee and Companionship

The Groundhog's Wisdom: Timeless Lessons for Modern Life

The Shadow Oracle: Groundhog Day as a Predictor

Emerging from the Burrow: A Journey of Renewal

The Language of Love: Learning Your Partner's Love Style

Authorpreneur: The Ultimate Blueprint for Writing, Publishing, and Thriving as an Author

Weathering the Seasons: Groundhog Day Perspectives

Valentine's Day Magic: A Guide to Romantic Rituals

The Shadow Chronicles: Stories of Groundhog Day

Love and Laughter: Fun Games for Valentine's Day

AstroRealty: Unlocking the Stars for Property Success

The Groundhog's Path: A Guide to Seasonal Balance

Groundhog Day Diaries: Reflections in the Shadow

The Groundhog's Light: Illuminating the Path Ahead

Valentine's Traditions from Around the World

AI Wealth Revolution: Unlocking the Trillionaire Mindset

Love Rekindled: Reigniting Passion in Relationships

Single and Thriving: Self-Love on Valentine's Day

Emerald Legends: Mystical Tales of Ireland

Green Alchemy: Harnessing Nature's Magic
The Hearts of Horror: A Valentine's Day Nightmare
The Leprechaun's Guide to Wealth and Wisdom
Dancing with the Sidhe: Celebrating the Otherworld
Shamrocks and Shadows: Mysteries of the Green Isle
Emerald Energy: Harnessing Luck and Growth
The Gingerbread Golem's Valentine: A Sweetheart's Guide to Love and Enchantment
The Celtic Knot: Weaving Life and Destiny
Green Fire: Elemental Magic for St. Patrick's Day
Clover Chronicles: Finding Your Inner Luck
Ireland's Mystical Creatures: A Field Guide
Gingerbread Golem's Love Almanac
Prowl and Thrive: The Lion's Guide to Success
Love Alchemy: Transforming Your Life Through Heart Energy
WORLD DOMINATION: Woman's Rule 3:The New Life
The Midnight Rose: A Guide to Lunar Love Spells
The Forbidden Letters: Writing Your Own Love Prophecy
Luck and Lore: St. Patrick's Day for Modern Mystics
The Green Path: A Pagan Celebration of Renewal
The Dark Architect's Guide to Reprogramming Reality
Prankster's Paradise: A Guide to Harmless Hijinks
Manifest Your Reality: The Law of Attraction Simplified
The TARDIS Owner's Manual: Understanding the Doctor's Ship: *A complete guide to the TARDIS, its technology, secrets, and mysteries*
Starlit Romance: Astrology Secrets for Finding True Love
The Time Lord's Atlas: A Complete Guide to the Whoniverse: ***A breakdown of the locations, planets, and dimensions explored in Doctor Who***
Sweetheart Shadows: The Dark Side of Love and Attraction
February Fire: Reigniting Passion in Every Area of Life

The Self-Love Toolkit: 5 Ways to Embrace Who You Are
February Sparks: Ignite Your Dreams in 28 Days
March to Success: A 31-Day Action Blueprint
Ancient Paths: The 13 Sacred Principles of Dino Wicca
Echoes of Tomorrow: Navigating the AI Revolution
The Wellness Blueprint: Balancing Mind, Body, and Soul
Green Horizons: Sustainable Living for a Better Tomorrow
The AI Wealth Code: How to Make Millions with Automation
AI-Powered Creativity: Writing, Art, and Music for Profit
Extinction Rites: Rebirthing Your Soul Through Prehistoric Magick
Sacred Serpents tarot
Celestial Enchantment blank journal
Star Strains
Culinary Journeys: Exploring Global Flavors at Home
The Hollowvale Curse
The Hollowvale Harvest
The Egg of Transformation: Awakening Your Inner Power
Blooming Into Power: A Wiccan Guide to Spring Awakening
The Nightmare Nexus: The Third Doctor's Perilous Haunting
Digital Detox: Reclaiming Your Life in a Connected World
Ostara's Path: Walking the Spiral of Renewal
The Sacred Hare
Financial Freedom: Building Wealth in the Modern Age
Spring's Cauldron: Stirring the Waters of Change
The Hollowvale Pact
Quantum Consciousness: The Science of Reality Shifting
The Hollowvale Hunger
The Sacred Waters Within: A Witch's Guide to Hydrocephalus Magick
The Raven's Nest: Building a Life of Unshakable Stability
AI and the Human Mind: The Future of Intelligence
The Hollowvale Reckoning

Timeless Love: Building and Maintaining Lasting Relationships

The Raven's Roar: Unlocking Unstoppable Confidence

Raven Sight: Awakening Intuition and Inner Wisdom

The Butterfly Effect: Small Changes, Big Transformations

Taming the Boogeyman: How to Conquer Your Inner Fears

The Magick of Green: Awakening Earth's Energy in You

The Entrepreneurial Mindset: Secrets to Business Success

The Hollowvale End

The Shadow Luck Ritual: Reclaiming Power from Your Dark Side

Spring Magick for Beginners: A Simple Guide to Seasonal Energy Work

Doctor Who: The Hollowvale Conundrum

The March of Miracles: Unlocking Synchronicities in Spring

Unveiling the Cosmos: A Guide to Stargazing and Space Exploration

The Ultimate Guide to Surviving an Economic Collapse

The AI Gold Rush: How to Profit from the AI Revolution

Bastet's Shadow: The Hidden Power of Feline Magick

The Bastet Codex: Unlocking the Goddess's Magickal Secrets

Purring Spells: Harnessing Bastet's Healing Frequencies

Bastet's Nine Lives: Rebirth, Transformation, and Immortality Spells

Primal Currents: Hydrocephalus Magick in the Path of Dino Wicca

The Digital Gold Rush: Mastering E-Commerce and Online Sales

Future Shock: Adapting to the Next Decade of Change

The Quantum Mindset: Think Like a Billionaire

Sacred Motherhood: Awakening the Divine Feminine Within

The Mother's Spellbook: Enchantments for Love, Protection, and Prosperity

The Witch's Guide to Parenting: Raising Empowered and Intuitive Children

The Magick of Motherhood: Reclaiming Your Power Through Rituals

The Pagan Path to Self-Love: A Goddess's Guide to Worth and Confidence

Wild Woman Magick: Unleashing Your Primal Power

The Money Magnet Blueprint: Unlocking Unlimited Wealth

Biohacking 101: Unlock Your Body's Full Potential

The Wild Father: A Pagan Guide to Strength and Wisdom

The Sacred Masculine: Unlocking Your Inner Power

The Druid's Compass

The Warrior's Mindset

The Father's Fire

Odin's Path

Ancestral Bonds

The House That Whispers

The Magician's Code

The Wild Hunt

The Green Man's Path

The Altar of Success

The Shadow and the Sword

The High Priestess's Guide to Energy Healing

The Lunar Mother

The Sacred Self-Care Grimoire

The Womb Wisdom Codex

The Wheel of the Mother

The Witch's Guide to Manifestation

The Q2 Reset

The Ultimate Guide to AI-Powered Passive Income

Escape the 9-5

AI Feline Fortunes

The Tear-Stained Grimoire

Razorblade Runes
Cemetery Sirens
The Midnight Wristwatch
The Town That Forgets
AI Horror & Creepypasta
The Hollow Frequency
The Breach Echo
The Quiet Between Worlds
The Sigil of Tharan-Khul
Summon the Vault of Y'ha'ten
The Becoming Codex
The Profit of Az'ra-nar
The Drowned Logos
Echoes of the Eldritch Will
The Deep Ledger
Necronomicon of Networth
Covenant of the Wealthwyrm
The Whisperer's Manifesto
The Rites of Azh-K'luth
The Ark of the Crawling Coin
The Tithe of Shadows
Inkheart Abyss
The Timewinds of Y'ha-nthlei
The Spiral Labyrinth of Azag-Nirrh
The Gallifreyan Heresy of the Black Pharaoh
The Psalms of Nyog-Sotha
Black Rain Alchemy
The Infinite Maw
The Entropic Blueprint
The Oracle of Sh'guul
The Book of Breach
The Drowned Saint's Testament
Dreamcraft of the Sleeper God

The Silence Market
Cthonomics: The Dark Wealth Algorithm
Invocation of the Ten-Eyed King
Wealthbound to the Wyrm Below
Become the Unnameable
Codex of the Sovereign Flame
Rituals of Relentless Becoming
The Shadow Ascends
The Eyes Beneath You
The Will That Wakes Worlds
Silence Is a Weapon
The Mirror That Screams
The Whisper Between Moments
The Mind That Devours Fear
The Myth of the Finished Self
The Architect of Your Madness
The Voice You've Buried
The Discipline of Madness
Stormborn: Awakening Your Inner Tempest
The Mind That Ate Time
Unbind Your Becoming
The Pact You Owe Yourself
The Devourer's Diet
The Acid That Carves the Path
The Tower You Must Burn
The Breath Between Worlds
Speak Like the Deep
The Labyrinth Within
The Spine of the Sea God
Rejection Is a Portal
The Crown You Refused
The Scar Is the Spell
The Lightless Flame

The Habit of Becoming Horrific
ChickenJockey Chaos
The Gatekeeper Within
You Are Not Your Name
The Compass of the Mad
The Archive of Unsent Letters
What the Mirror Can't Show You
The Knife You Needed
Worship Nothing, Become Everything
The Other Voice
The Body the World Forgot
The Vein of the Void
The Black Bone Codex
The Puzzle of the Hidden Self (Millennium Puzzle)
The Eye That Sees the Lie *(Millennium Eye)*
The Ring of Return (Millennium Ring)
The Rod of Relentless Will ***(Millennium Rod)***
The Tally of the Soul (Millennium Tauk/Necklace)
The Key to the Locked Timeline (Millennium Key)
The Scale of Sacred Decisions (Millennium Scales)
Inferno Bites: The UnOfficial Minecraft Lava Cookbook
Rot in the Attic
Prana: The Hidden Force of Your Infinite Self
The Shadow Realm Within: Transforming Darkness Into Destiny
The Borderland Collapse
Claws of Protection: Bastet's Defensive Magick
Mr. Ring-a-Ding's Madness
Yugioh Astrology: Celestial Deckcraft and Duel Destiny (2026–2027 Edition)
The Seal You Signed: Unlocking the Power You Once Feared
The Puzzle of Infinite Minds: Unlocking the Mentalism Hidden Within

Harnessed Minds: Breaking Free from Mental Control
The Eyes in the Smoke
Rootwake: The Carbon Covenant
Skitter Logic: Unlearning the Fear That Built You
Doctor Who: The World That Froths
Rootwake: The Fizz That Rewrites Flesh
Rootwake: Frothfather of the World
The Holly Pact: Blood Beneath the Mistletoe
The 2nd Mass Principle: Building Unbreakable Tribes
Web of Wits: A Survival Guide to Encounters with Anasi the Spider (Aunt Nancy)
The Hexbreaking Handbook: Effective Spells to Remove Curses
Pop Alchemy: Transform Your Life One Sip at a Time
The Mason Code: Leading in Unleadable Times
Petosiris and the Fifth Chamber of Thoth
The Ether Seed Within
The Parent of Tomorrow
Petosiris's Pyramid of Perpetual Wealth
Unlearn the World
Grimoire of the Hollow Tongue
Zodiac Weeds: Finding Your Strain Through the Stars
Aquarius Rises in the Bank
The Sugar God's Smile
The Skinclock Reversal: Biohacking the Face of Time
Debtburn: How to Obliterate What You Owe Forever
The Ice Cream Oracle: What Your Cone Says About Your Future
Silence Is Sovereignty: The Power of Being Unreadable
The Wind That Whispers Through Stone
Path of the Four Directions
Doctor Who: The Maestro's Symphony of Endings
Oxygen Grail: Breathing to Undo the Clock

Zodiacal Collapse: When Stars Devour Time
Teachings from the Red Sand Silence
Doctor Who: Omega – The Broken Equation
Memory Wipe Your Past: Start Over Like a MiB
Mitochondria Prime: Ignite the Core of Youth
A Nest of Roaches
Grub from the Galaxy: MiB Recipes You'll Never Forget
Whiskers of Power: Bastet's Guide to Inner Sovereignty
The Gift Must Cost Them: Negotiation Through Unequal Exchange
The Worm Guys' Wealth Code: Hustle Like an Alien
Bug Out: The Edgar Method for Ruthless Goal Setting
Weaving Life with Spiderwoman's Pattern
Doctor Who: The Rani's Renaissance
How to Get a Job (If You're a Puppygirl)
Speak Through Others: The Art of Proxy Power
T-Rex Your Trauma: Reclaim the Power of Your Primal Self
The Black Briefcase: How MiB Stay Wealthy in Silence
The Thirst Beyond Reason: Understanding Diabetes Insipidus From the Inside Out
Backwoods Witchcraft for Billionaires: The Pagan Path from Dirt Roads to Gold Roads
The Moonshine Grimoire: Fermented Spells for Abundance
The Nameless Geometry
The Wraith's Mixtape: Spellcasting with Songs of Sorrow
The Gallifreyan Gentleman: Silent Wealth, Sonic Confidence, and the Doctor's Code of Living
Sugar Water Confidence
Dino Totems: Spirit Guides from Earth's First Gods
Pumpkin Sigils & Ritual Smoke
The Hózhó Compass
The Distortus Discipline – Order from Inner Mutation
Witchcraft for the Cold-Blooded Soul

Moonlight Over the Blessingway
Water, Interrupted: When the Body Forgets How to Hold On
Deformed but Divine: Embracing Your Asymmetry
Hexes in the Henhouse: The Farm Witch's Guide to Power
The Reversed Flame: A Grimoire of Inverted Power
Salt, Cells, and Sanity: Reclaiming Balance with Diabetes Insipidus
King of the Broken: Crowning the Flawed Self
Moonlight Scars: Emo Moon Magick and the Art of Lunar Sorrow
Noose Spells: Magick of the Hanging Rope
The Goth Cathedral: Rituals of the Broken and Beautiful
The Cretaceous Codex: Dino Spirits and Fossil Magick
The Turkey Bones Ritual
Nine Lives of Manifestation: Unlocking Bastet's Reality Codes
Chaos Muscles: Building Strength from Twisted Pain
Emo Blood Magick: The Veins of Power
The 3AM Flood: Nighttime Urination, Sleep Loss, and the DI Spiral
The Silence Between the Stars
The Lemon Method: Sour Your Way to Success
Starlit Sovereign
The Rite of Twelve Gates: Walking the Gates of the Duat.
Cornbread and Conjure: Recipes for Riches and Rootwork
The Black Rose Rituals: Emo Love Spells and Obsession Magick
The Eternal Goodbye: Death Magick and Rebirth Rituals
Sinkrot: The Drain That Remembers
The Hybrid Mindset: Thinking Beyond Evolution
Bone Dry: Navigating Dehydration Before It Breaks You
Wreathcraft: Winter Sigils and Yuletide Spells
The Rite of Twelve Mouths

S'mores of the Damned: Haunted Recipes for Halloween Night

Rethink the Drink: A Beverage Survival Guide for DI Warriors

The Shadow Chord: Guitar Magick and Sonic

Malformed Yet Majestic: Leading When You Feel Wrong Inside

The Cursed Diary: Ink-Stained Spells of the Emo Soul

Anxiety Off Switch: Emergency Reset for a Fried Nervous System

The Energy Heist: How to Take Back Your Life from Drainers

Beyond the Bathroom: Rebuilding Your Social Life With DI

Coyote's Gift for Decision Makers

Ghoul-Goo: Spooky S'mores You'll Die For

Echoes in the Mirror: Scrying and Self-Destruction Magick

Thread and Thorn: Stitching Spells from Rural Cloth

The Mogwai Mind: Building Untouchable Wealth from Small Ideas

Be Your Own Guide: Trust Your Inner Compass

Hormones in Chaos: The Endocrine Puzzle of Diabetes Insipidus

ChronoCleanse: Detox Your Biological Timeline

The Limb You Hide Is the One That Saves You

Leaves, Bones, and Whisper Spells

The Dinosaur Mindset: Prehistoric Tactics for Modern Wealth

Clawing Back Control: A Bastet Method for Boundaries and Empowerment

Samhain Codes of the Forgotten

Orange Alchemy: The Autumnal Spellbook

Monster Within, Master Without

The Sigil That Sleeps

Hearthcraft: Yule Hearth Sigils and Winter Warmth Spells

Temple of the Purring Moon: Rituals from Bastet's Lineage
When the Earth Remembers Your Footsteps
Food for Mood: Eat to Heal Depression, Not Just Survive It
Witch of the Kudzu Vine: Southern Pagan Wealth Secrets
The Invisible Diagnosis: Advocating for Yourself With DI
The Coffin's Lullaby: Sleep Magick and Nightmares as Portals
Ashes of the Will: Rituals for Erasing the Self
The Fracture Rite: Shattering the Magickal Core
Funeral Candles: The Art of Emo Flame Magick
The Black Grimoire: A Blank Ritual for Writing in Absence
Phantom Thirst: A Halloween Survival Guide for Diabetes Insipidus
The Hollow Crown: Emo Royalty and Magick of the Outcast King
Sandpainting for the Soul
Falling Into Balance: Using the Extra Hour to Recalibrate Life
100 Southern Superstitions That Still Work
The DI Child: A Parent's Guide to Raising Hydrated, Happy Kids
The Jungle of Shame: Escaping the Hidden Lab of Doubt
The Witch's Toast: S'mores Spells and Creepy Confections
The Hoodoo Pantry: Spells from the Mason Jar
The Immortal Fortune: Secret Wealth Lessons from Captain Jack Harkness
The Specter's Embrace: Magick for Channeling Ghostly Lovers
Grateful Waters: A Thanksgiving Survival Guide for Diabetes Insipidus
The Seizure Gospel
Harvestbind: Autumn Sigils and Samhain Spells
Doctor Who: The Algorithmic Awakening
Silent Nights, Steady Waters: A Christmas Survival Guide for Diabetes Insipidus

The Extra Hour Effect: How One Hour Can Transform Everything

Blade Between the Breaths

Running with the Mountain Shadows

Echoes of the Failed Experiment – Becoming a Living Legacy

Swamp Witches & River Ghosts: Real Southern Hauntings

Cornbread Prophecies: Magical Recipes from a Southern Table

Doctor Who: The Signal in the Star

Bloomcraft: Spring Sigils and Equinox Enchantments

Vanisher: How to Disappear from the Internet Without Losing Your Life

The Ultimate Christmas Cookie Cookbook

The Unbreakable Parent: How to Mentally Survive Raising Kids in a Broken World

Time Debt: How to Reclaim the Hours You Didn't Know You Lost

One Month, One Million: Unconventional Cash Creation Tactics

Doctor Who: The Cyber Conversion Protocol

Black Friday Frenzy: The Art of Finding Hidden Online Deals

The Grimoire Buried Under the Apple Tree

Digital Couponing Masterclass: Your Step-by-Step Guide to Black Friday Savings

The Fire Inside the Flint

Shadows on the Ceiling: The Emo Guide to Astral Magick

The Bone-Eaters Beneath Us

Black Friday Bundle Blueprint: Creating Irresistible Product Packages for Maximum Sales

Thirteen Nights of Unbinding

Doctor Who: Engines of Influence

Pumpkin Spice Alchemy: Recipes of Fire and Frost

When Raptor Met Rexy: Prehistoric Lessons in Wild Romance
Oblivion's Candle: Burn the Path Behind You
Campfire Curses and Chocolate: A Halloween S'mores Grimoire
The Wallet That Wasn't Mine: Breaking Free from Inherited Scarcity
The Cola Zodiac: What Your Fizz Says About Your Fate
Frostfire Fortune: Unlocking Winter's Hidden Prosperity
Signal Jamming: Detox Your Brain from Info Overload
The Dust of the Forgotten Rite
The Golden Cat Sigils: Drawing Power in Bastet's Name
Mud Magick: The Prosperity of Getting Dirty
Savory Spicefall: Beyond the Pumpkin Pie
Pumpkin Spice Apothecary Kitchen
The Pumpkin Spice Economy: Turning Trends into Billions
The Ember Veil: 13 Nights of Fire Magick
Financial Freeze: When Earning Triggers Panic
The Gingerbread Alchemist: Sweet Recipes with a Twist
Biosynth Power: Programming Yourself from Scratch
Echoes from the Talking Circle
Truffle Alchemy: Fungus of Fortune
Spores of Power: The Truffle Witch's Handbook
Doctor Who: The Tower That Speaks
The Mycelium Veil: Truffle Magick Unbound
Broke But Ashamed: Healing the Shame Wound of Debt
The Evergreen Mind: Growth Through Winter Stillness
The Black Veil Truffle Rite
The Voice Beneath Symbols
Witchlight on the Bayou: Swamp Spells for Sovereignty
I Grew Up Poor and Now I Sabotage My Success
The Lantern of Hollow Souls

Shutdown Survival: A Citizen's Guide to Thriving When Government Stops

When Abundance Feels Like a Threat: Healing the Hidden Fears of Enough

The Scarecrow Grimoire

Owls of the October Veil

Candlewax and Curses: A Halloween Spellbook

Excavating the Inner Fossil – Transforming Fossilized Thoughtforms into Tools of Power

The Yule Witch's Spellbook: Magick for the Holiday Season

Haunted Christmas: Ghost Stories for Winter Nights

The Christmas Survival Guide: Thriving Through the Chaos

The Bone Orchard Rites

Haunted Commerce: The Ghost in the Marketplace

When Money Triggers the Inner Child

Silent Night with the Silence: A Christmas Thriller

The Lightning Crown: Living and Leading Through Seizures

TARDIS Tidings: Festive Stories from the Whoniverse

Autumn Reset: Slowing Down Without Falling Behind

The Trillion Dollar Soul: Rewriting the Currency of Reality

Truffle Eclipse Magick

Micro-Manifestations: Quick Magick That Works

5-Minute Rituals for Busy Witches

The Marshmallow Massacre: Halloween Treats with a Sinister Twist

Blood and Blackberry Thorns

Magickal Mornings: Rituals for a Blessed Christmas Day

Embers of the All-Hallows Fire

The Pumpkin Market Collapse

The Hour You Gained: Transforming Time Into Power

The Chamber Must Be Sealed: Mastering the Power of Controlled Access

The Cursed Manuscript of Petosiris

The Festive Hearth: Creating Holiday Traditions
Darkness Rising: Thriving as Nights Grow Longer
Harvesting Time: Turning the Year's End Into Your New Beginning
Petosiris and the 13th Zodiac Key
Wagewound: When Paychecks Become Identity Prisons
Walls That Watch
The Silent Feast: Rituals of Power in the Longest Night
The Distortus Legacy : Becoming a Deformed King in a Perfect World
The Hollow Masks
The Gratitude Furnace: Forging Gold from Thanks
Feast of Inner Gold: Eating for Energy and Enlightenment
Haunted Commerce: The Season of Spending Spirits
Fear Bonds: How Panic Creates Profit
Black Friday E-Commerce Playbook: Sales Tactics to Skyrocket Your Holiday Revenue
Budgeting for Black Friday: A Holiday Savings Planner
Haunting the Harvest Moon
The Warrior's Water: Emergency Preparedness for People With DI
The First Sip of the Year: A New Year's Survival Guide for Diabetes Insipidus
Doctor Who: The Thirteenth Node
The Unseen Struggle: Mental Health, Anxiety, and Chronic Thirst
The Hearth's Hidden Ledger: Counting Energies as Currency
The Gift Alchemist: Turning Any Offering Into Gold
The Papyrus of the Bound Spirit
The Magick of Leftovers: Transmutation in the Fridge
Frost and Fortune: Christmas Wealthcraft for the Modern Magus
Last-Minute Gifts: Creative Ideas on a Budget

10 Secrets to Surviving Holiday Crowds
The Witch's Dow Jones
The Witches' Graveyard Shift
Pumpkin Sigils: Carving Rites for Midnight Power
The Secret Shopper's Black Friday Guide: How to Get Early Access and VIP Deals
Fever in the Foundation
The Neuralyzer Reset: Reprogram Your Morning Routine
Lightning Lessons of the White Painted Woman
The Enchanted Snowflake
The Magic Sip: Surviving Disney Parks with Diabetes Insipidus
The One Who Draws Through You
Santa's Secrets: A Magical Holiday Planner
Silent Bells, Loud Miracles: Self-Help for the Season of Stillness
The Sugar Spell Codex: Confectionary Magick of Christmas
Autumn Hexcraft: Fallen Leaves, Fallen Barriers
Sleep Like a Fortress: Build a Life Where Insomnia Can't Survive
Nowhere Was Ever Home
Christmas Under the Stars: A Celestial Holiday Guide
Rentproof: How to Never Be Evicted Again
Workless: Escape the 9-5 Without Being Broke
The Gilded Gift: A Wealth Altar for Christmas Morning
The Black Friday Grimoire
The Hollowing: Ceremonies of Spiritual Collapse
Doctor Who: The Nameless Signal
Where the Eagle Hides His Courage
The Dwarf Tyrant's Ascent: Claiming Power in a World of Giants
The Currency of the Dead: Trading with Spectral Bankers
The Icebound Witch: Survival and Magick in the Cold

The Emergency Money Mind: Constant Crisis, Zero Calm

Thirst & Roses: A Valentine's Survival Guide for Diabetes Insipidus

Springing Into Clarity: Mastering the Energy Shift of Daylight Saving

Speed of the Nanotyrant: Agile Strategies for Life's Hunt

The 90-Day Reset: A Science-Backed Guide to Reinvent Yourself Before the New Year

The Coil of Thorns

Timegates Unleashed

Dopamine Fasting 2.0: Rewiring Your Brain in a World of Overstimulation

The Nanotyrannus Mutation: Embracing Your Differentiated Form

Unwritten January: How to Use the Blank Page of the Year to Re-Author Your Life

Feast of the Forgotten Spirits: Ancestor Magick for the Holidays

The Burnout Codex: A System for Thriving Beyond Stress

I Don't Deserve to Have Money

When the King Doesn't See You: The Shadow Predator's Guide

The Reset Ritual :A Guide to Shedding Last Year's Weight—Emotional and Physical—by Spring Cleaning Your Soul

Calendar Alchemy: Learn to Bend Time and Productivity around Your Natural Rhythms

The Mirror Contract: A One-Sentence Agreement with Yourself that Unlocks Real Change

The Nile Formula: Sacred Flow for Millionaire Minds

Forward Momentum: Productivity Rituals for the Lost Hour

Harvest Gold: Wealth Magick of Pumpkin Spice Commerce

The Magick of Christmas Lights: Illuminating Holiday Rituals

Cranberry Crown: Royal Self-Worth through Ritual Meals
Petosiris and the Worms of the Feathered Throne
The Evergreen Equation: Self-Help for Sustained Growth
The Rain Will Wash Us Away: Emo Weather Magick
Snowlight Shadows: Magick Under Frozen Stars
Doctor Who: Merger of Empires
The Light Within the Feast: Magickal Wealth of Yuletide Flame
Momentum Machines: Small Habits Designed to Snowball into Unstoppable Forward Motion
Calm Spells: Magickal Solutions for Anxiety Relief
Santa's Final List: The Naughty Never Leave
The Mystic's Guide to Banishing Worry
The Silence Dividend: Turning Quiet Mornings into Compounding Growth All Year
Charmed Stillness: Rituals to Ease the Mind
Blood Spiral Ascension
The Vanishing Heart Invocation
Crystal Calm: Harnessing Stones for Anxiety
The Nano Tyrant Code: Strength in the Small Predator
The Energy Ledger: Accounting Methods for Vitality, Not Just Money
Snowglobe Mindset: Shake Up Your Thoughts, Settle Into Peace
The Weight of the Feather: Anubis's Codes for Soul Balance
Pocket Peppermint Power: Tiny Rituals for Big Holiday Energy
Shadowkeeper of the Golden Jackal: Anubis's Path to Energetic Protection
The Witch's Breath: Anxiety Relief Through Magickal Breathing
The Tiny Ember: Pocket Motivation for Cold Days

The Twelfth Doctor: The Rebel with a Cause (Peter Capaldi, 2013–2017)

The Thirteenth Doctor: Breaking the Mold

(Jodie Whittaker, 2017–2022)

The Fourteenth Doctor: A New Beginning (David Tennant, 2022–2023)

The Fifteenth Doctor: Rewriting the Stars

(Ncuti Gatwa, 2023–2025)

Santa's Shortcut to Success: Micro Habits for a Better New Year

The Midnight Cocoa Manifesto: Comfort Rituals for Hard Nights

Why I Can't Save: Trauma Blocks to Financial Planning

Dino Brain, Mega Goals: Rewire Yourself for Savage Success.

Jurassic Profit: Unearth Your Inner Millionaire Fossil

Scales & Softness: Dating with Dino Heart

Carnotaurus Dreams.

Red Willow Thinking.

Reindeer Resilience: How to Keep Going When You're Exhausted

Candlewick Courage: Lighting Strength in Dark Seasons.

Elf-Mode Focus: Fast Attention Fixes for Busy Seasons

Futureproof Feelings: Emotional Skill-Building for Resilience No Matter What the New Year Brings

The 90-Day Rewire: Transform Your Neural Pathways Before Spring Blooms

Jolly Rich: Christmas Micro-Money Magick for Fast Prosperity.

Gingerbread Gratitude: Mini Practices for a Happier Holiday

Trauma-Spending: When Money Becomes a Drug

Goal Skeletons: Build Minimalist Frameworks for Resolutions That Last

The Snarl Strategy: Growling Back at a World That Silenced You

The Hourglass Reset: Reclaiming What the Clock Took

Yule Claw: Dino Rites of Light in the Darkness

Sacred Circles: Grounding Rituals for Anxious Souls

Clockstopper's Gut: Rebuilding the Core of Time

Winterfire Drive: Harness the Cold Season's Stillness to Ignite Deep Motivation

The 5-Minute Productivity Hack: Small Steps to Big Results

Light Ascending: A Self-Help Guide to Longer Days

Inner Economy: Trade Self-Doubt for Confidence Like a High-Value Currency

Simple Success: Decluttering Your Life for Better Results

The Resilient Mind: Thriving in Tough Times

The 2026 Playbook: Mastering the Year Ahead

The Spring Sleep Solution: Conquering Fatigue After Time Change.

The Hormonal Compass: Navigate Back to Your Youth

Golden Vision: Eating for Your Eye Color with the Power of Ghee

Lionhearted Love: Strength in Relationships

MiB Mindset: Think Like a Cosmic Agent

The Ladder of Small Wins: Climb Out of Stagnation by Stacking Micro-Victories

The Momentum Hour: Gaining More in Less Time.

The Year of You: A Self-Help Blueprint for Unapologetic Self-Ownership

The Dust That Watches You Back.

The Astral Parent

Shadow of the King: The Nanotyrannus Parable

Tiny Tidings of Triumph: Small Wins That Change Your Life

Dwarf Tyrant Rising: When You're the One They Overlook

The Bank Account Mirror: Healing How You See Yourself Through Money

Cretaceous Black

When Love Costs Too Much: Romantic Triggers and Financial Wounds

Get Some Tarot cards: https://www.makeplayingcards.com/sell/apophis-occult-shop

Get some shirts: https://www.bonfire.com/store/apophis-shirt-emporium/

Instagrams:
@apophis_enterprises,
@apophisbookemporium,
@apophisscardshop
Twitter: @apophisenterpr1
Tiktok:@apophisenterprise
Youtube: @sg1fan23477
Hive: @sg1fan23477
CheeLee: @SG1fan23477

Podcast: Apophis Chat Zone: https://open.spotify.com/show/5zXbrCLEV2xzCp8ybrfHsk?si=fb4d4fdbdce44dec

Newsletter: https://apophiss-newsletter-27c897.beehiiv.com/

If you want to support me or see posts of other projects that I have come over to: **buymeacoffee.com/mpetchinskg**

I post there daily several times a day

Get your Dinowicca or Christmas themed digital products, especially Santa Raptor songs and other musics. Here: **https://sg1fan23477.gumroad.com**

Apophis Yuletide Digital has not only digital Christmas items, but it will have all things with Dinowicca as well as other Digital products.

www.ingramcontent.com/pod-product-compliance
Lightning Source LLC
LaVergne TN
LVHW022221200926
848481LV00006B/2065